THE MEDAL FROM HEAVEN

and

Other Saints Stories for Kids

Melaine Ryther

To David, Nick, Emily and Lucy.

Table of Contents

Introduction   3

St. Catherine and the Medal from Heaven   5

St. Martin and the Monastery Mice   9

St. Isidore's Angel   14

St. Francis and the Wolf   18

St. Rose and the Pirates   23

The Angels of the Alps   28

About the Author   33

Acknowledgments

"St. Isidore's Angel" was previously published in *My Friend Magazine*, September 1996.

"St. Catherine and the Medal from Heaven" was previously published in *My Friend Magazine*, May 1997.

"St. Martin and the Monastery Mice" was previously published in *My Friend Magazine*, April 2004.

My Friend Magazine was a monthly Catholic publication for children, owned and operated by Pauline Press and Media. Sadly, it is no longer in operation.

INTRODUCTION

In writing these stories I have taken certain liberties with settings and dialogue in an effort to make the accounts read like, well, stories, instead of chapters from a dry and dusty textbook. It is a technique often used by authors when retelling legends. It makes the material fresh and entertaining, as well as informative.

While miracles and wonders are fun to read about, I encourage you to remember this first and foremost: the saints are our friends and are always available to hear our prayers. Their lives have been recorded through the ages so we can strive to imitate them. They loved God and their neighbors, acted heroically, and left us beautiful examples of how we can do the same.

Just one more quick thing. It's really not a good idea to try to imitate *everything* the saints did, like fending off pirates and talking to wolves. If you're unsure, check with your parents.

Enjoy.

M.R.

ST. CATHERINE AND THE MEDAL FROM HEAVEN

"Sister! Sister! Sister!"

An urgent voice woke Catherine Labouré from her deep sleep. She blinked several times. Radiant light filled her convent bedroom. The light came from a beautiful child about five years old, dressed in white. "Come to the chapel," said the child. "The Blessed Virgin is waiting for you there."

Obediently, the young Sister of Charity followed the child. She marveled as the chapel door, usually locked, opened at a mere touch of the child's fingertips. Entering the sanctuary, Catherine heard the rustling of silk. She looked toward the altar and beheld a beautiful woman seating herself in a chair. The child told her, "This is the Blessed Virgin."

Catherine, who had lost her own mother at an early age, threw herself at the feet of her heavenly Mother and placed her hands in her lap. How could this be happening to me? she wondered. This is 1830 France!

"My child," said the Blessed Virgin, "the good God wishes to charge you with a mission."

Overwhelmed with joy, Catherine listened to all that the Mother of God had to tell her. France would undergo many political and religious turmoils, warned Our Lady. But throughout those and other difficulties, anyone who asked for graces at the foot of the altar would be granted them.

Two hours later, Catherine watched with sweet sadness as the Blessed Mother disappeared from sight. Only later did she realize that she had not learned what her "mission" was to be. She trusted that God would reveal it eventually. Four months later, He did.

* * *

On November 27, 1830, while praying alone in the chapel, Catherine heard the familiar rustling sound again. Turning her head to look, she saw the Blessed Virgin standing near a picture of St. Joseph. Rays of light, symbolizing graces, streamed forth from rings on all her fingers. She stood on a globe, crushing the head of a serpent under her feet. Then slowly an oval frame appeared around her, on which were written the words: "O Mary, conceived without sin, pray for us who have recourse to thee."

At the same time a voice said to Catherine, "Have a medal struck after this model. All who wear it in confidence will receive great graces. They should wear it around the neck."

Then the apparition turned around, revealing what the back of the medal was to look like. Catherine saw a large M in the middle of the oval. Above the M were a cross and bar. Beneath the M were the hearts of Jesus and Mary. One was crowned with thorns; the other pierced by a sword. Encircling all of this were twelve stars. Then the apparition vanished.

In obedience to Mary's instructions, Catherine told only her confessor, Father Aladel, about the apparitions. Catherine really wanted to please Our Lady, but she would have to wait almost two years before the Archbishop of Paris granted permission for the first medal to be made. Soon after people began wearing the medal, healings, conversions and favors of all kinds began to happen. Before long, the medal had a new name, the "Miraculous Medal."

In spite of the many extraordinary events taking place around her, Catherine's life after the visions remained quite ordinary. The sisters who lived with her never guessed she had been the one who had seen the Blessed Virgin. Catherine spent the next forty-six years caring for the elderly and sick. Only when she was close to death, after first obtaining permission from Our Lady, did she tell the others that Mary had appeared to her.

* * *

Today the chapel where the apparitions occurred is one of the most popular religious shrines in the world. They even still have the blue velvet chair in which Mary seated herself during her apparition. Millions of people around the globe wear the Miraculous Medal as a testimony to their faith and the power of trusting prayer.

ST. MARTIN AND THE MONASTERY MICE

"Where is Brother Martin?" demanded the young Spaniard. He held up a bed sheet to show the curious monks who had gathered around. "There are more holes in this sheet than in a cobbler's workbench!"

Martin de Porres put down his broom and quickly went into the hall upon hearing all the commotion.

"I'm sorry about the sheets, Roberto," said Martin. "The mice must have gotten in the linen closet again."

"Do you think so?" asked Roberto sarcastically. "Listen here, I've had it with the animals and the beggars and all the other vermin you insist on bringing into this monastery. I am studying to be a priest, not an innkeeper!" He threw the tattered sheet into Martin's arms and stormed off down the hall.

Father Miguel, the monastery's superior, came over to Martin. "You must forgive Roberto for the way he speaks to you. His family is one of the wealthiest in Lima and employs many servants. He has much yet to learn."

Martin smiled and shrugged. Roberto's meanness didn't bother him. The son of a Spanish knight and a black Panamanian woman, Martin was well aware that many considered him lower class because of his dark skin. But Martin also knew that all people, even those who rejected him, were his brothers and sisters. He bore their prejudices patiently, in imitation of Jesus, who was also shunned and humiliated.

"Perhaps," continued Father Miguel, "we should do something about the mice, though. At this rate we may soon find ourselves sleeping on straw." Father Miguel chuckled and gave Martin a friendly wave goodbye.

Martin quickly finished his sweeping while his mind formulated a plan. Father may have been joking, but Martin viewed the chewed-up sheets as no laughing matter.

* * *

Holy Rosary monastery was eerily quiet as the clock ticked closer to midnight. Martin sat on the cold concrete floor facing the linen closet, trying desperately to stay awake. He had worked harder than usual that day. In addition to his normal housekeeping duties, two of the brothers had come down with fevers and needed Martin's doctoring skills.

While not a true physician, Martin was a trained barber. And in the sixteenth century, a barber not only cut hair, but also administered medicine, set broken bones, and even pulled teeth! Though at times the work was demanding, Martin loved the opportunities his vocation gave him to serve others.

A faint scratching noise brought Martin to attention. A tiny shadow crossed in front of his gaze. Martin held his breath, focused—and pounced!

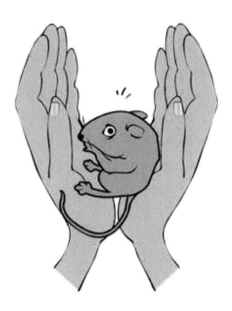

"Aha!" He felt the frightened mouse tremble in his hands. "Don't be afraid," Martin said as he stroked the little creature's fur. He bent close and spoke softly to it: "Now then, you will be my messenger. Tell your friends they must not eat the clothes in this closet anymore. The next brother to catch them may not be as understanding as I am. Here is what I propose. If you fellows will stay out of the closet, I will feed you every day in the garden out back."

The mouse wrinkled its nose and twitched its whiskers, but Martin was confident it understood what he was saying. He knew that God had given him a special gift, that of being able to communicate with animals. He let the anxious creature go and watched it scoot behind the closet door.

Not more than ten minutes went by when the walls all around Martin began to stir with activity. Scratching and squeaking echoed from every corner of the monastery. Several bedroom doors opened as sleepy monks came out to investigate.

"What is all that racket?" demanded Roberto, rubbing his eyes.

Before Martin could answer, dozens upon dozens of mice appeared from every direction. Some waddled while others raced down the hall toward the garden. As he dashed off after them to keep his end of the bargain, Martin called over his shoulder to Roberto: "Your sheets will stay intact now, brother. Just don't sleep in the garden!"

* * *

St. Martin de Porres was born in 1579 in Lima, Peru. He began training as a barber's apprentice at age 12. By the time he joined the Dominicans at age 16, his holiness was evident to all who met him. Martin had a great love for the poor and the oppressed, and for all of God's creatures, great and small. He died in 1639 of a severe fever. St. Martin is the patron saint of interracial justice as well as of barbers.

ST. ISIDORE'S ANGEL

"Senor de Vergas, you must dismiss Isidore at once!" The angry foreman struck his sombrero against his leg, scattering dust in every direction.

"And what is the problem this time?" asked Juan de Vergas wearily.

"He is late for work every morning. And he talks out loud to no one! The other workers are upset. With the harvest upon, Senor, we can't allow one man to cause such a disruption!"

Juan de Vergas listened carefully to his foreman's complaint. This wasn't the first time he had heard stories about his gentle laborer. It was rumored that on holidays Isidore would go into Madrid and seek out the poorest inhabitants, sharing his meager food and belongings with them. Despite Isidore's odd reputation, his work was always done to satisfaction, often above and beyond. But now Juan de Vergas faced a more serious situation. If Isidore's behavior was affecting the other workers, something needed to be done.

"I will take care of it, Miguel," he said.

* * *

The next morning, Juan de Vergas arose from bed at 4:00 a.m. and walked across his great estate to Isidore's small shack, where he hid himself behind a tree. It wasn't long before Isidore came out, walking quickly through the darkness, past his employer, and down the dirt road leading to the neighboring village.

After following Isidore for a mile, Juan de Vergas spotted the steeple of the village church and watched as Isidore entered. He decided to wait. Mass wouldn't last that long.

And it didn't. About forty minutes later a handful of villagers filed out of the small church. Isidore's employer looked earnestly for his humble farmer among the passing faces, but nowhere did he see Isidore. Quietly he peered inside the church. There was Isidore, hands clasped together reverently, eyes focused on the altar. His lips were moving, though he was alone in the dimly lit sanctuary. This man has great faith, though Juan de Vergas. He returned to the estate house, leaving Isidore to pray.

The next morning, he followed Isidore to the church again. Once more Isidore remained behind after Mass had ended. His employer could not bear to disturb him. Juan decided instead to go to the fields. Perhaps he could explain Isidore's zeal to the others and convince them to be patient with their co-worker. He sought out Miguel.

"The workers are very happy, Senor," reported the foreman. "Whatever you said to Isidore seems to be working. He has been the first one in the fields, and has more than doubled his plowing the last two mornings."

Juan de Vergas stared at his foreman in disbelief. How could that be?!

Determined to find an answer, the following morning he followed Isidore to the small church again. But this time, instead of waiting for the Mass to end, he raced to the fields as soon as Isidore entered the building.

Only one laborer was out plowing at that early hour.

Surely that cannot be Isidore, thought Juan de Vergas. Yet those are his oxen.

He approached the lone figure in the field, making his way carefully through the early morning mist. Suddenly the fog cleared, and he stopped abruptly. For in front of him passed a strikingly handsome young man dressed all in white, with hair more golden than the surrounding wheat, and a face more radiant than the sun's reflection. As he guided the oxen past the startled farm owner, the young man's feet seemed to float over the ground. Despite the strange and unknown sight before him, Juan de Vergas was filled with peace and joy.

* * *

St. Isidore the Farmer was born in Madrid, Spain, in 1080 A.D. Because of his parents' extreme poverty, he went to work for Juan de Vergas at a very young age, and remained with him the rest of his life. Isidore's holiness was witnessed by many, and in 1622 he was formally canonized a saint. St. Isidore is the patron saint of Madrid, as well as of laborers of all the world. His symbol is a sickle.

ST. FRANCIS AND THE WOLF

"My Stefano!" wailed the old woman. "No, no, no! Not Stefano!"

Francis walked over to where a crowd had gathered close to the gates of the city. As it was near evening, many of the men held lit torches. Light from the flickering flames revealed that many more brandished swords, longbows, axes, and clubs.

"What is going on?" Francis asked a white-haired beggar whom he had befriended just days earlier.

"The wolf," said the beggar. "The wolf killed the old woman's son."

Francis heard a man's deep voice rise up from the crowd. "We must hunt this beast! Who is with me?"

More voices answered back.

"The wolf is too strong!"

"It is a devil wolf!"

The first man's voice answered back: "So we stay prisoners in our own city? We allow it to eat our livestock, to keep us from our fields? Do you all want to starve?"

Francis moved forward and shouted above the angry murmurs. "Friends! Citizens of Gubbio! Please listen. You have been most kind for letting me stay in your fine city. Allow me to return the favor by meeting with this wolf and securing peace between you."

"He is mad!"

"Crazy as the birds he preaches to!"

Francis was used to ridicule. He knew how strange it appeared when he spoke out loud to animals. But God had given him a special gift, one that allowed him to show that all creatures are capable of giving praise to their Creator.

"He is not mad, he is a man of God," said a gruff voice. All heads turned to see a brown-robed friar step out of the crowd. "Brother Francis, I will go with you."

Francis smiled at the friar. "Thank you, brother. God will protect us."

* * *

The next morning Francis and the friar set out. Some of the townspeople started out with them, but few had the courage to go any farther when the woods deepened and the shadows darkened.

Francis and his companion pressed on. They had seen wolf tracks in the soft dirt and knew it wouldn't be long now before they faced their adversary. They were soon proven right.

Snarling, jaws open wide, the wolf sprang out from behind a large rock. Francis quickly made the Sign of the Cross in the wolf's direction. To the amazement of the few who lingered nearby, the beast immediately stopped his charge.

"Brother Wolf, come to me," commanded Francis. "I order you, in the name of Christ, not to hurt anyone."

The wolf trotted over to Francis, lowered its head, and meekly lay down at his feet.

"Now then, Brother Wolf, you must stop terrorizing the people of this land. Not only have you attacked their animals, but you have dared to attack and kill humans, who are made in the image of God, their Creator and yours."

By now the timid townspeople had gathered closer, in awe of what they were seeing and hearing.

"I want to make peace between you and the people," continued Francis. "If you pledge not to harm them anymore, I promise that you will be fed every day and no longer hated and hunted." Then Francis stretched out his hand toward the wolf. "Will you make this pledge?"

The wolf extended his front paw and placed it in Francis's hand.

Francis smiled at the wolf. "All past crimes will be forgiven. But now you must come with me to town and make this pledge to the people of Gubbio."

The wolf followed Francis to town like a docile lamb. They entered the city's gates and stood in the marketplace, saint and wolf side-by-side. A massive crowd had assembled upon hearing the remarkable reports from the forest.

"Friends, we are here to make public our pledge for peace. Brother Wolf will not hurt you or your animals, and in return you will feed him every day. Do you agree?"

"Yes!" cheered the crowd.

"Brother Wolf?" asked Francis.

As it did in the woods, the wolf shook his body in agreement and then lifted his paw toward Francis's outstretched hand.

For two years after the pact was made, the wolf lived among the townspeople, going door to door for food each day. The wolf harmed no one, and no one harmed it. When the wolf finally died of old age, the people of Gubbio were genuinely sad. They had lost their living reminder of the wonders and holiness of St. Francis. But in their hearts they still retained their faith and love of a timeless and powerful God.

* * *

St. Francis of Assisi is the patron saint of animals and of Italy. He is famous for working miracles, obtaining conversions, and being the first saint to receive the stigmata (the wounds of Christ on one's own body). St. Francis is one of the most revered religious figures in history.

ST. ROSE AND THE PIRATES

"They're coming!" sputtered the old man between coughs. "I tried to tell the viceroy's men that I saw them from my boat. They wouldn't believe me!"

Rose gave his hand a gentle squeeze and promised she'd be back with a soothing cup of herbal tea. She made her way through the infirmary that was also her home, stopping every few feet to give out food, medicine, or comfort. She prayed silently that God would protect all of Lima's citizens, from the poorest Indian to the wealthiest Spaniard. Rose knew the old fisherman was right. Her guardian angel had told her the same thing two nights ago.

The pirates were coming.

* * *

From earliest childhood, Rose felt a special calling from God. She frequently experienced visions of her guardian angel, St. Catherine of Siena, and the Blessed Virgin. At age 20, she entered the Third Order of St. Dominic, a religious order for lay people. This choice allowed her to live at home and help support her family, which she did by selling exquisite needlework and homegrown flowers.

Rose also had a consuming desire to look after the poor and sick, especially children and seniors. With her parents' blessing, she opened a room of their house to use as a shelter, where Rose provided medical care with herbs grown in the family garden. It wasn't long before stories spread far and wide of miraculous cures obtained through Rose's prayers.

* * *

"Sister Rose! They're here! They're here!"

Startled by the loud shout at the doorway, Rose dropped her teacup and turned to see the frightened face of twelve-year-old Eduardo. His family often bought Rose's flowers to sell in their store.

"The pirates are here! They are destroying everything! They . . . they hurt my papa!" Eduardo's face shattered, tears gushing down his face as he dropped to the ground in a heap.

Rose rushed to him. Embracing him tightly, she whispered in his ear, "Eduardo, listen carefully. You must be brave and get the children to follow you to the church. I will take as many of the others as I can." She tilted his head up to meet her gaze. "God will take care of us, child, but you must act quickly. Do you understand?"

Eduardo nodded and raced off, his tears wet on Rose's sleeve.

"Jesus, protect us," Rose said under her breath, then moved quickly to round up her people.

* * *

The Church of Santo Domingo was filled to capacity. Standing at the front of the church near the altar, Rose could see the fear in people's faces and hear their panic-tinged voices. Many had heard the same news as Rose: the pirates were deliberately searching for churches to destroy in their violent frenzy.

"We are doomed!" came a shout from the back.

"You have led us to our death!" came another.

"Listen everyone!" Rose commanded. "We must trust in God and pray like we have never prayed before!"

Led by Rose, the crowd settled into a rhythm of prayer, their voices praising and petitioning as one, when suddenly a thunderous boom filled the air.

All heads turned to the back of the church. In the gaping hole where the doors used to stand were a throng of bloodied and wild-eyed men. The biggest and ugliest strode forward, sword in hand and hate in his eyes.

"Where is your God now?" he snarled.

"He is here!"

The pirate looked up and stopped in his tracks as he beheld a young woman ablaze in light, holding above her head a golden monstrance containing the Blessed Sacrament. The crowd watched, mesmerized, as Rose slowly walked toward the pirates.

"Begone! In the name of Jesus Christ, leave our land and people alone!"

The head pirate dropped his sword from his trembling hand, clumsily backed up a few steps, then turned and fled from the church. The other pirates ran after him.

Amazed onlookers throughout the city watched as hordes of pirates suddenly stopped their pillaging and plundering and returned to their ships, as if commanded by some unseen force.

Soon their ships were distant dots on the horizon, leaving the citizens of Lima to rejoice and praise God.

Back in the church, Rose found Eduardo and put her arm around him. "Come, my friend, we have much work to do."

* * *

St. Rose continued to serve the poor and sick of Lima until her own death at the early age of 31. Stories of her miracles, conversions, visions and other wonders were so abundant that she was declared a saint within her own generation's lifetime. St. Rose of Lima is the first canonized saint of the Americas and is the patron saint of Peru. She is often pictured wearing a wreath of roses and thorns.

THE ANGELS OF THE ALPS

The loud thud at the heavy wooden door made Brother Antoine bounce up to a sitting position on his narrow cot.

"Yes, yes, coming," he warbled, wondering just how long he had been asleep. The wind was howling much worse, he noted, than when he had first started his gatekeeper's shift.

With a mighty effort he pulled open the door, just enough for a snow-covered figure to lumber inside and fall in a heap on the floor.

"Friend . . . help," gasped the stranger. "My friend needs help!"

Brother Antoine wasted no time. He reached up and rang the bells. An emergency was at hand!

"Get the dogs ready," Brother Antoine instructed the responding monks. He prayed silently that they would reach the other traveler in time. As the treacherous south wind battered the aged hospice walls, he was reminded just how ripe the conditions were for avalanches this high in the Swiss Alps.

* * *

"Over that way!"

"I hear it!"

Despite the fearsome din of the alpine winds, the barking was unmistakable to the two monks. They skied along the icy mountain ledge toward the waiting dogs.

"Good boy! Keep him warm, Albert," said Brother Michael, as he readied the ropes on the rescue sled. Albert, a massive 200-pound Saint Bernard, was snuggled close to a still, wool-clad young man.

Brother Girard swished over seconds later. He reached for a canteen of warm tea. "That's it, Madeline, wake him up now," he said to the second, smaller Saint Bernard. The dog was busily licking the frozen man's face.

Within moments the man groaned and blinked at the droopy-faced dogs hovering over him. Madeline waved her bushy tail, delighted that a new friend would soon be going home with her.

* * *

Later that night, the two weary travelers huddled close to the fireplace under several layers of blankets. Their gaze alternated between the flickering flames of the fire and the portrait of a rugged-looking man above the mantle.

Brother Antoine walked in with a tray of tea and saw the men's interest in the picture. "St. Bernard of Menthon," Brother Antoine declared. "He was a very holy priest who spent forty years of his life in these mountains preaching the Gospel. In 1050 he founded our monastery and hospice to provide a shelter for travelers crossing the pass." He cast a smile toward his guests. "Such as yourselves."

"He lo-lo-looks like a true mountaineer," the first man remarked between chattering teeth.

"He was a strong man, indeed. And fearless as well," Brother Antoine said. "He single-handedly drove hordes of bandits out of these mountains. Yet he could also be as gentle as a lamb."

"Li-li-like his dogs, wouldn't you say, Father?"

"Very much. But the dogs came up here long after

Bernard. They were a gift from the neighboring nobles in the seventeenth century."

"And they have been rescuing people ever since?" the second man asked.

"Yes and no. Originally the dogs served as companions and watchdogs for our brothers. It wasn't long, however, before they discovered what wonderful pathfinders the dogs are. Or just how sharp their senses are. Do you know a Saint can pick up a scent that's hours old?"

The monk paused to sip his tea. He looked at the man whose teeth were chattering. "You, my friend, were buried under three feet of snow. But you could have been covered with seven feet and the dogs would have found you!"

Brother Antoine set his cup down. Then, with a gleam in his eye, he asked the men, "Do you know what their greatest quality is?"

The two men shook their heads no.

"They are a constant reminder of God's own goodness. If only all creatures would show such charity and sacrifice. They bring great honor to their Creator."

And with that final thought, Brother Antoine excused himself from the travelers' company to put the Saints to sleep.

* * *

God's Search and Rescue Team

Did you know that Saint Bernards . . .

. . . have been specially bred to withstand harsh winters? Their thick, short fur protects them against the cold and ice. And their large, well-padded paws enable them to "swim" through the snow.

. . . are able to sense avalanches and earthquakes? They feel the rumblings under the earth and are therefore able to alert others of the coming danger.

. . . were at one time used by the Augustinian priests to "cook" in the hospice's kitchen? They were fitted with special harnesses that allowed the dogs to turn spits of roasting meat.

. . . never carried casks of brandy around their necks? They are often posed that way, however, for tourists looking for a good photograph.

. . . have reportedly saved over 2,000 people since records were first kept at the hospice? Barry I, the most famous Saint Bernard dog of all time, saved over 40 lives alone between 1800 and 1812.

ABOUT THE AUTHOR

Melaine Ryther has been writing for kids and adults since the mid-1990s. Her work has appeared in a variety of magazines, including *My Friend, Boys' Life, National Geographic World, Catholic Parent, Catholic Heritage, Columbia, Woman's World, Country Woman*, and many more. She lives in Washington State with her husband and children.

Made in the USA
Middletown, DE
16 November 2021